Kielburger

Champion for Children's Rights and Youth Activism

Linda Barghoorn

Crabtree Publishing Company
www.crabtreebooks.com

Author: Linda Barghoorn

Series research and development: Reagan Miller

Editorial director: Kathy Middleton

Editor: Crystal Sikkens

Proofreader: Wendy Scavuzzo

Photo researchers: Samara Parent and Crystal Sikkens

Designer and prepress technician: Samara Parent

Print coordinator: Margaret Amy Salter

Photographs:
Alamy: © WENN Ltd: page 21

The Canadian Press: © Moe Doiron: page 6; © AP/Gunnar Ask : page 8; © Tom Hanson: pages 13, 14

Getty Images: © Paul Zimmerman: cover; © Jim Bennett: title page; © Jason Kempin: pages 4-5; © Dominik Magdziak Photography: page 7; © Patti Gower: page 10; © Bernard Weil: page 11; © John van Hasselt - Corbis: page 12; © George Pimentel: pages 20, 28; © Steve Jennings: pages 22-23; © Anthony Harvey: page 24; © Michael Tran: page 25; © Mat Hayward: pages 26-27

Keystone Press: © Free the Children/TCS/ZUMA: pages 15, 16, 17, 18; © wenn.com: page 29

Shutterstock.com: © Yavuz Sariyildiz: page 9; © thomas koch: page 19

Wikimedia Commons: © ARamhit: page 30

All other images from Shutterstock

About the author: Linda Barghoorn grew up in Fonthill, Ontario and attended Brock University in St. Catharines, where she graduated with a Bachelor of Arts in German. She spent twenty years living outside Canada – in Europe and the Middle East – during which time she began writing about and photographing her experiences. She is married with two grown daughters, and lives and works in Toronto, Canada.

Library and Archives Canada Cataloguing in Publication

Barghoorn, Linda, author
    Craig Kielburger : champion for children's rights and youth activism / Linda Barghoorn.

(Remarkable lives revealed)
Includes index.
Issued in print and electronic formats.
ISBN 978-0-7787-3420-8 (hardback).—
ISBN 978-0-7787-3424-6 (paperback).--
ISBN 978-1-4271-1919-3 (html)

    1. Kielburger, Craig, 1982- --Juvenile literature. 2. Children's rights--Juvenile literature. 3. Humanitarianism--Juvenile literature. 4. Human rights workers--Canada--Biography--Juvenile literature. 5. Thornhill (Ont.)--Biography--Juvenile literature. I. Title.

HQ789.B374 2017   j323.3'52092   C2016-907101-4
                                    C2016-907102-2

Library of Congress Cataloging-in-Publication Data

CIP available at the Library of Congress.

Crabtree Publishing Company

www.crabtreebooks.com   1-800-387-7650

Printed in Canada/022017/CH20161214

Published in Canada
Crabtree Publishing
616 Welland Ave.
St. Catharines, Ontario
L2M 5V6

Published inthe United States
Crabtree Publishing
PMB 59051
350 Fifth Ave., 59th Floor
New York, NY 10118

Published in theUnited Kingdom
Crabtree Publishing
Maritime House
Basin Road North, Hove
BN41 1WR

Published in Australia
Crabtree Publishing
3 Charles Street
Coburg North
VIC, 3058

Contents

Craig Kielburger

We can learn a lot from each other by sharing stories of our lives. A story of a person's life is known as a biography. Some people's stories are considered remarkable. They may involve bravery, inspiration, or kindness. Craig Kielburger (KEEL-ber-ger) has qualities that many people find remarkable. He is a **humanitarian** and social **activist** who is caring, committed, and passionate.

What Is a Biography?

We read biographies to learn about a person's experiences and thoughts. Biographies can be based on many sources of information. Primary sources include a person's own words or pictures. Secondary sources include friends, family, media, and research.

One Person Making a Difference

Since he was 12 years old, Craig has demonstrated that it is possible for each of us, as global citizens, to make a difference. His compassion and dedication have inspired others to become better individuals by reaching out to help people in need. He has united young people around the world in a movement for change. As you read Craig's story, think about the qualities that have made his achievements possible.

? THINK ABOUT IT

Do you know a remarkable person? What qualities do you admire about them?

*Craig has dedicated his life to helping **impoverished** children, and to empower all children to play a role in shaping the world they live in.*

Learning About Child Labor

Craig with his father, Fred. Fred and his wife Theresa inspired their children to be confident and **inquisitive**.

Craig was born on December 17, 1982. He lived with his parents, Theresa and Fred Kielburger, and older brother Marc, in Thornhill—a neighborhood near Toronto, Canada. Both his parents were teachers. They encouraged their boys to be caring toward others, and to follow their hearts to find a purpose in life.

Just Like Any Kid

Craig was like any other Canadian kid growing up. He loved reading science fiction and was involved in Boy Scouts. He attended summer camps and enjoyed being with his friends. He looked up to his older brother Marc as a role model. He admired Marc's passion for environmental activism and wanted to follow in his footsteps. When Craig was just 12 years old, he read a newspaper story about a young boy his age on the other side of the world. That story changed his life.

> 66
>
> *The first person who showed me it doesn't matter how old you are to make a change was my older brother, Marc.*
>
> —Craig Kielburger, Myhero.com. Peacemaker Hero: Craig Kielburger, 2013
>
> 99

Craig, left, always looked up to his older brother Marc as a role model.

Iqbal Masih

Craig was in seventh grade when he read about Iqbal (ICK-bal) Masih (Ma-SEE). Iqbal had been a young boy in Pakistan. He was just four years old when his family sold him to a carpet weaver for twelve dollars to pay a debt they owed. Iqbal was taken from his family, chained to a loom, or weaving machine, and forced to make carpets. He became a slave, or child laborer, who would never earn enough money to pay for his freedom. When he was ten, he escaped and began to raise awareness about child labor. Unfortunately, he was killed when he was 12 years old for speaking out.

Iqbal Masih became a child laborer who would never earn enough money to pay for his freedom.

Child Laborers

Child laborers are children who are forced to work instead of attending school. Often the work is dangerous and can cause them to become sick or injured. Experts think there are almost 170 million child laborers in the world. More than five million of these children are **forced laborers** or slaves. About one million children perform unsafe work in underground mines, and more than half of all child laborers work on farms.

These children in Turkey are forced to work in cotton fields instead of going to school.

An Activist Is Born

Craig was also 12 years old when he discovered Iqbal's story. He was shocked that two 12-year-old boys on the same planet could have such different lives. He wanted to find out more about child labor and what he could do about it. He asked his classmates to help him. A small group of friends, including his brother Marc, volunteered. They met at the Kielburgers' house and began to study the issue and how they could help.

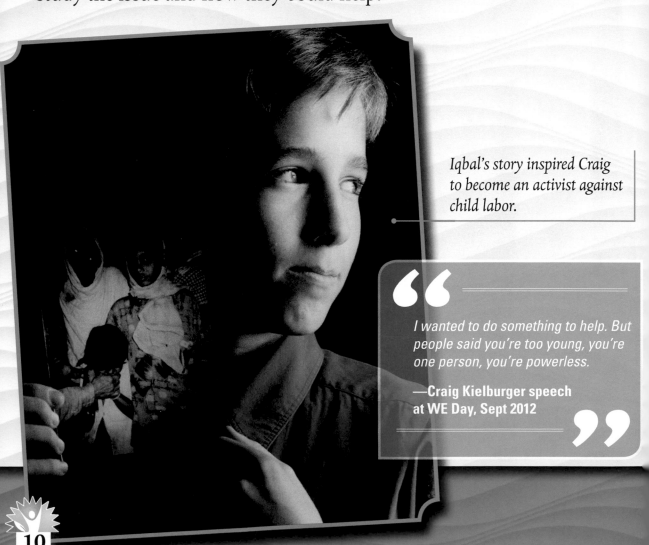

Iqbal's story inspired Craig to become an activist against child labor.

"

I wanted to do something to help. But people said you're too young, you're one person, you're powerless.

—Craig Kielburger speech at WE Day, Sept 2012

"

Too Young to Help?

As Craig learned more about child labor in many countries, he became determined to stop it. But he couldn't find a charity that would let him get involved. Everyone told him he was too young. Craig insisted on playing an active role to find solutions. After all, who could understand children's problems better than other children like himself? Although he was sometimes discouraged, Craig kept going. Finally, he and Marc decided to create their own charity so they could write their own rules for change.

? THINK ABOUT IT

What obstacle did Craig face as he tried to take action?

Craig worked hard to raise awareness about child labor.

First Steps

Craig and Marc named their charity Free The Children. They continued to do research to educate themselves about child labor and **exploitation**. Craig organized car washes, garage sales, and bake sales to raise money to support their work. He visited nearby schools to encourage other children to join his **campaign**. He sent faxes to world leaders begging them to act. He signed **petitions** against child labor and supporting human rights.

Human Rights

Kailash Satyarthi is a human rights activist in India who has helped lead a global campaign to end child labor. He was arrested and put in jail by the government for his efforts to stop carpet factory owners from using child laborers.

Craig helped collect 3,000 signatures on a petition sent to the Prime Minister of India, demanding Kailash (KI-lahsh) Satyarthi's (Saht-ee-YAHR-tee) release.

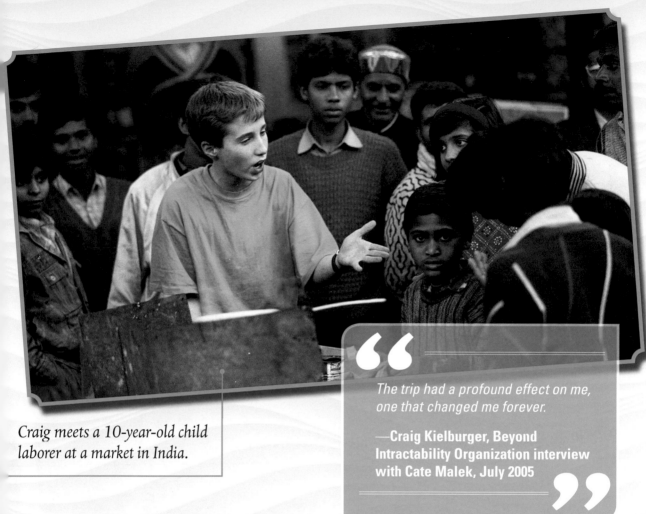

Craig meets a 10-year-old child laborer at a market in India.

> "
> The trip had a profound effect on me, one that changed me forever.
>
> —**Craig Kielburger, Beyond Intractability Organization interview with Cate Malek, July 2005**
> "

Face to Face

Craig wanted to see firsthand what the lives of child laborers were like. After months of trying to convince his parents to let him take time off school so he could travel, they finally agreed. Accompanied by a young adult from Bangladesh, Craig spent seven weeks traveling through India, Pakistan, Thailand, Nepal, and Bangladesh. He visited **slums** and factories, where he met children living in extreme poverty and being exploited as child laborers.

Building a Charity

Craig said he found real heroes in the **vulnerable** children he met in Asia. Despite their poverty and exploitation, they refused to give up hope for a better life. While in India, Craig asked for a meeting with the visiting Canadian prime minister. While the prime minister did not offer to support Craig's work, their meeting helped raise awareness of the child labor issue in Canada and around the world. People started noticing Craig and the work he was doing. He was featured on television shows. Children sent coins taped to postcards as donations. His charity began to grow quickly.

Craig meets with Canadian prime minister, Jean Chrétien, during his tour through Asia.

Early Efforts

Free The Children began organizing adult teams to raid factories, fields, and quarries in poor communities to find child laborers. They then arranged to return these children to their families. But, often the children's families were too poor to feed and take care of them. The children were later sold into slavery again, or a brother or sister was sold in their place. Free The Children found themselves rescuing the same children more than once. Their plan wasn't working.

? THINK ABOUT IT

What problem did Free The Children's teams encounter when returning child laborers to their families?

An enthusiastic team of young people helps run Free The Children from their headquarters in Toronto. It has become the largest children's rights charity in the world.

Building Schools

Craig realized they needed a different strategy. He asked for ideas from the children they had rescued, their families, and local community groups. They proposed that child labor would only stop when the poverty faced by their families was eliminated. They proposed that better schools would allow the children to get an education and grow up to earn better jobs. Craig decided to change his charity's **mission**. They would turn their efforts to community development. They began building schools in Nicaragua, Kenya, Ecuador, and India.

> *If child labor is wrong for a white, middle class child in North America, then why is it any different for a girl in Thailand or a boy in Brazil?*
>
> **—Craig Kielburger, Reebok Human Rights Award speech, 1996**

Craig helps build a new school in India with a team of volunteers.

Adopt a Village

Soon Craig discovered that still more was needed. Impoverished families couldn't afford to keep their children in school. Without the children working to support their families, there wasn't enough money for food, housing, and education. Craig's charity looked for new solutions. They developed a strategy of support called Adopt a Village. Through this program, staff from Free The Children work with local community members and governments to create programs, which help build strong, independent communities. Money for these programs is raised through international donations until the village can support itself.

Craig helps students with their lessons in their new classroom in a village in Kenya.

Tools for Change

The Adopt a Village program addressed many issues faced by impoverished communities. Nutrition programs, farm training, seeds for planting, and **irrigation** systems helped families to establish reliable food sources. Adults were provided with leadership sessions, training, and workshops to help create better job opportunities. Along with education, members of the local community worked together to build wells to provide clean water for drinking and farming. They established medical clinics, and delivered training and supplies to provide proper health care to the community.

Craig takes time out from work in Kenya to play with the children.

Empowering Communities

Many charities deal with humanitarian emergencies by offering short-term solutions. They repair villages after an earthquake, or help feed communities during a drought. But they often don't stay long enough to help poor communities achieve long-term change that will improve their futures. Craig's charity takes a different approach. It **empowers** communities to become active participants in their development, instead of just accepting help from outsiders.

? **THINK ABOUT IT**

How is Craig's charity different from other charities?

Earthquake victims receive food and temporary shelter until their homes can be rebuilt.

The WE Movement

Craig is determined to create a world in which every child can receive an education. From a young age, he learned that real happiness comes from helping others. He felt most inspired and happy when he saw his work change the life of an exploited child. He wants other children to experience this sense of fulfillment. While some of his overseas programs require adult training and support, Craig works tirelessly to empower children to help other children.

New Name

Free The Children is now known as the WE Movement. Its motto is: "I pledge to live WE by making a difference, every day."

Craig believes strongly in the three C's: compassion, courage, and community.

From ME to WE

Craig's determination, energy, and enthusiasm have helped him build a youth movement that connects communities around the world. He believes that the power to make big change comes from many small individual acts of kindness. When many "Me's" act, "WE" can make big changes happen. His organization is a wonderful example of the enormous power of individuals to change the world when they unite in a shared cause.

? THINK ABOUT IT

What does the phrase "when many Me's act, WE can make big changes happen" mean to you?

Craig speaks at a national ME to WE Day in Toronto, Canada.

WE Beliefs

Several beliefs inspire the WE Movement's work:

- WE is each individual whose efforts inspire others to act.
- WE is a movement of individuals with unique talents who can achieve more by working together.
- WE is a global community with connections that span the world.
- WE exist for one reason: to create a better world for everyone.

> " The purpose of our group is not only to free children from exploitation and abuse but also to free children from the idea that they are powerless and have no role to play in today's society.
>
> —**Craig Kielburger,** *In Search of Character* **video series:** *Free The Children*, **2009** "

Craig enjoys speaking with high school students to inspire them to become active and involved citizens.

WE Schools

To encourage more children to participate in service projects, the WE Schools program was created. A one-year classroom program teaches students about global poverty, hunger, and education issues. They receive educational materials, a monthly schedule, and access to speakers and helpers who can support their work. During the year, they must complete one local and one global **service project**. Students also learn leadership, writing, and critical-thinking skills, which will help them become active and engaged citizens.

> " If you give kids the inspiration and the tools to change the world it will change their own lives in the process.
>
> —**Craig Kielburger, *60 Minutes* interview with Ed Bradley, 1996** "

Girls' education activists Shiza Shahid and Malala Yousafzai joined Craig Kielburger to help celebrate England's first WE Day.

WE Day

Craig is passionate about inspiring youth by recognizing their achievements. He helped develop WE Day to celebrate young peoples' efforts to create a better world. WE Day takes place in 14 cities across the United States, Canada, and the United Kingdom. More than 200,000 students attend each year. It is an exciting day of music, speeches, and awards. Motivational speakers, dynamic performers, and committed activists come together in a concert-like event to celebrate change and energize further action.

You Can't Buy a Ticket

You can't buy a ticket to WE Day. You have to earn an invitation by participating in at least one local and global service project. Projects could include collecting food for a local **food bank**, books for a library in an underprivileged community, or raising money to support a medical clinic overseas. WE Day can be a life-changing event. It unites thousands of young people in celebration, and reminds them they are not alone in their efforts to change the world.

> WE Day isn't just a day. WE Day is a movement. A movement that happens all year long.
>
> —**Craig Kielburger speech at WE Day, September 2012**

Many famous celebrities, including Selena Gomez (below), Demi Lovato, Joe Jonas, Gord Downie, and Nelly Furtado, have participated in WE Day.

The International Stage

Craig's charity has grown from a small group of school friends to a network of more than 100,000 youth in more than 35 countries. Craig spends much of the year traveling the world. He visits projects in different countries, speaks at conferences and schools, leads WE Days, and meets with people who support his work. Craig has a newspaper column in which he shares tips about **socially conscious** living. He has published 12 books. His first—*Free The Children*—was written when he was 16 and described his trip to Asia as a 12-year-old.

A Big Heart

While continuing his charity work, Craig completed university degrees in peace and conflict studies and business. But he remains, most importantly, a dedicated activist for children's rights. Craig has been inspired by great leaders such as Mother Teresa and Nelson Mandela (Man-DELL-ah). And he has shared meals with impoverished families struggling for survival in the world's poorest countries. Known for his selflessness and big heart, Craig has many friends, supporters, and admirers.

NELSON MANDELA

Heroes

Mother Teresa was a Catholic nun and **missionary** adored by millions for her lifelong charity work. Nelson Mandela inspired the world with his fight against **apartheid** in South Africa.

WE Days give young people a chance to learn more about humanitarians around the world.

Recognition and Awards

Craig Kielburger has received countless awards. In 2006, he was honored with the World Children's Prize, which recognizes outstanding children's rights heroes. In 2008, he was made a member of the Order of Canada. This award celebrates exceptional achievement and service to the country. His work has been featured on TV shows, including *The Oprah Winfrey Show* and the *National Geographic*.

Wedding Bells

In June 2016, Craig married Leysa (LEE-sah) Cerswell (KERS-well). They had a socially conscious wedding at which guests brought photos with a hand-written personal message instead of gifts. Leysa wore an ethically sourced diamond and guests threw wild flowers instead of rice.

Craig and Marc are welcomed into Canada's Walk of Fame, which celebrates Canadians who have made special contributions to their country.

> Our parents… showed us that life is so much more than making a living—it's about the **legacy** we leave.
>
> —Craig Kielburger, We.org interview with Marc and Craig Kielburger

After 20 years, Craig and his brother Marc still continue to work side by side helping impoverished children and communities.

Amazing Results

Craig's enthusiasm, commitment, and leadership have delivered some amazing results. His charity has built more than 650 schools overseas, given one million people access to clean water, raised $45 million for projects worldwide, and logged more than 20 million volunteer hours. He has promised to continue his charity work until there is no more work to be done.

Writing Prompts

1. Did you know that slavery still exists and that children are often its victims? What have you learned about slavery while reading this book?

2. Craig was determined to show that a 12-year-old could help change the world. What skills did he use in his work to raise awareness about child labor?

3. Craig uses a "ME to WE" strategy to unite young people to help create change. How does this work? Why is it effective?

4. What are some of the most important issues in helping to end poverty and child labor?

5. What kind of actions can you take in your daily life to play a role in Craig's youth movement?

Learning More

Books

It Takes a Child by Craig Kielburger. ME to WE, 2009.

Take Action! A Guide to Active Citizenship by Craig Kielburger & Marc Kielburger. Wiley, 2002.

My Grandma Follows Me on Twitter by Craig Kielburger & Marc Kielburger. ME to WE, 2012.

Websites

www.we.org
A comprehensive website outlining the work of Craig and Marc Kielburger, and their We Movement.

http://myhero.com/hero.asp?hero=c_kielburger
Peacemaker Heroes outlines the work of young peacemakers such as Craig Kielburger. It has a Recommended Reading section for further information on the subject.

http://stopchildlabor.org
The Child Labor Coalition works to end child labor exploitation. The website gives detailed information about the organization and current child exploitation issues around the world.

www.unicef.com
UNICEF works internationally to ensure the rights of children globally. Their website tells stories of the difficulties faced by children around the world, and UNICEF's work to help improve their lives.

www.hrw.org/topic/childrens-rights/child-labor
Human Rights Watch highlights issues affecting human rights around the world. This website explores the issue of child labor through articles and videos from a diverse list of countries.

Glossary

activist A person who uses strong actions to help make changes to society

apartheid A policy in South Africa which gave black people fewer rights than white people and forced them to live separately, often in poverty

campaign A set of activities or actions aimed at achieving a certain goal

empower To give power to someone

ethically sourced Something that is obtained in a way that is legal, safe, and does not harm anyone

exploitation The unfair and unsafe use of a person or thing

food bank A place that provides free food for poor people

forced laborer Someone who is forced to work in conditions that may be unsafe and for which they are often underpaid

humanitarian A person who works to make other people's lives better

impoverished Living in poverty; poor

inquisitive Describing a person who is curious and enjoys investigating things and ideas

irrigation An artificial system used to supply water to fields

legacy Something that is the result of someone's actions in the past

mission A task that is considered very important

missionary A person who helps people who are sick or poor

petition A document that people sign to show they want they want action or change

service project A volunteer project that supports a social cause

slum An area in a city where buildings are in poor condition and people live in poverty

socially conscious A way of acting or living that protects the rights of people and the environment

vulnerable Easily harmed in a physical, mental, or emotional way

Index